This book belo

MW01716992

Oh,no! What happened to the letters?!

First published in the United States of America by Kindle Direct Publishing.

First Edition

ISBN 979-8-9895710-0-0

Manufactured in United States of America

Book Cover by Rami Al Hakim
Illustrations by Rami Al Hakim

Oh, no! What happened to the letters?!

By Nikola Kovacic and Auntie Seka
Published by Kindle Direct Publishing

Oh, no! What happened to letter A?

Letter A ate too much!
It's time to lay down and rest.

Oh, no! What happened to letter B?

Letter B is bossy!
It's time to work together.

Oh, no! What happened to letter C?

Letter C got a cut!
It's time to be careful.

Oh, no! What happened to letter D?

Letter D got doubled!
It's time to be a twin.

Oh, no! What happened to letter E?

Letter E is egocentric!
It's time to think of others.

Oh, no! What happened to letter F?

Letter F fell down!
It's time to get up.

Oh, no! What happened to letter G?

Letter G is gassy! It's time to go to the bathroom.

Oh, no! What happened to letter H?

Letter H is hungry!
It's time to eat.

Oh, no! What happened to letter I?

Letter I is ill!
It's time to get some rest.

Oh, no! What happened to letter J?

Letter J is joking!
It's time to be serious.

Oh, no! What happened to letter K?

Letter K is a know-it-all!
It's time to learn from others.

Oh, no! What happened to letter L?

Letter L is lazy! It's time to do some work and help out.

Oh, no! What happened to letter M?

Letter M is mad!
It's time to calm down.

Oh, no! What happened to letter N?

Letter N is noisy!
It's time to be quiet.

Oh, no! What happened to letter O?

Letter O had an oops!
It's time to pay attention.

Oh, no! What happened to letter P?

Letter P is panicky!
It's time to take deep breaths.

Oh, no! What happened to letter Q?

Letter Q is quiet!
It's time to talk.

Oh, no! What happened to letter R?

Letter R is rebellious!
It's time to follow the rules.

Oh, no! What happened to letter S?

Letter S is scared!
It's time for some comfort.

Oh, no! What happened to letter T?

Letter T is tardy!
It's time to be on time.

Oh, no! What happened to letter U?

Letter U is uncaring!
It's time to be considerate.

Oh, no! What happened to letter V?

Letter V is vain!
It's time to be humble.

Oh, no! What happened to letter W?

Letter W is wonky!
It's time to find some balance.

Oh, no! What happened to letter X?

Letter X broke his xylophone!
It's time to fix it.

Oh, no! What happened to letter Y?

Letter Y is yawning!
It's time to get some sleep.

Oh, no! What happened to letter Z?

Letter Z is zippy!
It's time to slow down.

Made in the USA
Las Vegas, NV
20 April 2025

21137191R00019